JOY OF MY JOURNEY with JESUS

AND HOW A LEAP OF FAITH CHANGED MY LIFE

WRITTEN BY
DR. JOHN W. PEOPLES

EDITED BY
KAREN REDLACK

The Joy Of My Journey With Jesus: *And How A Leap Of Faith Changed My Life*

Book cover design and interior layout provided by Self Publish Me, LLC, Publishing Consulting and Book Design Services for Independent Authors. www.selfpublishme.com | email: info@selfpublishme.com

DEDICATION

I dedicate this book to my mother, Veta Jenkins Peoples, in memoriam; my children Marlon Vincente' Peoples, Roslyn Demetrice Peoples, John W. Peoples III; my grandsons, Donovan Peoples-Jones of Detroit, Michigan; Maury Wong Peoples of Toronto, Ontario, Canada; and to the matriarch of my family, Ms. Statia Marylyn Peoples-Rector of Oklahoma City, Oklahoma; my nephew Charles Peoples and my niece Lisa Peoples-Hammond of Oklahoma City, Oklahoma; my nephews Richard Peoples of Denver, Colorado; Kenneth Peoples of Boston, Massachusetts; Lawrence Peoples of Tulsa, Oklahoma; all of their children, grandchildren and future generations of my family.

TABLE OF CONTENTS

Introduction

March 10, 1953, the 17 year-old Johnnie Peoples, born in Oklahoma City, Oklahoma, boarded a Greyhound bus in Oklahoma City, headed to Detroit, Michigan, with only $30.00 in his pocket. When he arrived in Detroit, he had $29.95, having spent .05 for a soft drink at a bus stop in Terre Haute, Indiana. Johnnie had no relatives in Detroit, nor did he know anyone there. He carried an elegant looking gray and green suitcase which his mother had purchased for him exclusively for this journey. She also carefully packed a box full of food which included pork chops, fried chicken and peanut butter and jelly sandwiches.

On boarding the Greyhound bus, Johnnie headed straight for the rear section of the bus. He was aware that only White people could sit in the seats in the front and middle section of the bus. That meant even if there were available seats in the front of the bus, the segregation laws of the land forced Johnnie, and all "Colored" people to have to either sit in the rear of the bus or stand. Hence, Johnnie went to the rear of the bus.

It must be pointed out that the few seats in the rear of the bus designated for "Colored" were located just above the hot, extremely loud sounding and smelly diesel engine. The rear seats were also located above the rear wheels which means that passengers riding in the back of the bus could feel every bump on the highway.

Johnnie headed straight to the rear of the bus to find that the only seat available was between two rather "hefty" Colored women. With his box of food in hand, he was able to squeeze in between the two women.

After 12-15 hours and more than 500 miles of uncomfortable riding, the bus arrived in Terre Haute, Indiana for a scheduled stop to pick up passengers headed north. Johnnie decided this was a good time for him to get off the bus, stretch his legs and get something cold to drink. He went into the bus station and bought a bottle of pop. Upon returning to the bus he noticed there were a lot of empty seats available in the front section of the bus. He also reasoned that they had probably crossed the Mason Dixon Line (an imaginary geographical point that separated the segregated South from the integrated North) which meant he could now sit at the front of the bus. He took a wide seat, two or three seats from the front of the bus. At last, he had enough room to stretch out his legs and relax. He thought, now I can get some sleep!

At that very moment, he noticed a rather slender Colored man boarding the bus. The man stopped and looked around the bus at all the vacant seats. "Instead of taking one of those vacant seats," exclaimed Johnnie, "he took a seat right next to me. This made me so angry, I didn't know what to do, because I had planned to sleep the rest of the way to Detroit, although I didn't know how much farther it was, and what was even worse is that this stranger wanted to talk to me."

Looking back, Johnnie now realizes this was an angel

CHAPTER 1
IN THE BEGINNING

"Being raised during the Great Depression, World War II and the Jim Crow Era was rough, but you just had to make do with what you had."
—John W. Peoples (JWP)

In the middle of the Jim Crow Era and the Great Depression, Johnnie Peoples was born on December 5, 1934. He was in good company as two other historic and well-known African Americans, Hank Aaron and Bill Russell, were born earlier that same year. Aaron was a major league baseball player who played with the New York Giants and Russell played basketball with the Boston Celtics. Franklin Delano Roosevelt, the 32nd President of the United States was in his second term of office.

Times were hard in Oklahoma, as it was

all over the country, when Johnnie was born. It was just after the Second World War and the country was in a great economic depression.

At that time, the northern City limits of Oklahoma City was 23rd Street. Johnnie lived two miles farther north of 23rd Street on 50th and Bryant Street. Bryant Street is a mile east of what is now Martin Luther King Boulevard, but was then known as Eastern Avenue. A whopping three miles of Eastern Avenue is now known as Martin Luther King Boulevard. "In my opinion," comments Johnnie on this gesture, "renaming such a short stretch of the street was only meant as an attempt to pacify African Americans in the community."

Johnnie recalls the rural area where he lived on the southwest corner of 50th and Bryant Street was called the "country". His father and mother owned two acres of land where they grew everything they ate except flour, sugar, cornmeal and cereal. His father and mother had built the house shortly after they were married in 1914. The house where Johnnie lived had a basement, which was just a large hole in the ground, over which the little three room house was built. This hole in the ground served as a place where food items were kept in order to keep them cool; his parents had no "icebox". Electricity was not available to people who lived in the rural area; consequently, there was no refrigeration. In those days most people living in the rural area preserved their home grown food by a process known as "home canning". Vegetables were partially cooked and then placed in glass jars known as mason jars. The top of the jar was then sealed with a rubber seal under the jar cap. Women made their own clothes. In fact, they made everything but their shoes.

During the Second World War food and

petroleum was rationed. This meant that you could only purchase a limited amount of food items and gasoline. The government issued commodity stamps for food items and gasoline. You could only buy a certain amount of meat, sugar and flour. During the economic depression of the twenties and followed by World War II, people could only buy a small amount of meat, sugar, flour and gasoline. Sugar being a refined process, people would often extract syrup from trees and use that as a sweetener. Some farmers would raise "sugar cane" from which you could also extract the sweetness from the sugar cane to use as a sweetener. Very few people had automobiles. If you did own a vehicle, you could only purchase two gallons of gasoline for the entire month. Needless to say, people didn't drive very much.

Many African Americans living in Oklahoma City lived in an area referred to as the Fairground. This was bordered by

1st Street on the South and 23rd Street on the North; Lottie on the West and Eastern (now Martin Luther King) on the East. There were very few paved streets and very little electricity or water, even in the "city" part of Oklahoma City. Kerosene lamps and candles were used for lighting. There were very few indoor bathrooms in the city and none in the rural areas. What we called "out houses" or places where you could relieve yourself were stationed all over the city.

As difficult and as simple as those times were, they were wonderful days, and young Johnnie learned a lot. He learned to make bird houses, rabbit traps, shoe horses, and to be creative.

People had to make do with what they had.

Chapter 2
The Family

"My mother wasn't that strict, but all four of us kids were disciplined." —JWP

Johnnie's parents were John W. Peoples Sr. and Veta Jenkins. His father passed when he was only two years old; he never got a chance to know him. His mother was born in 1898. She had a good education; she attended Langston University, and even taught at Langston University. Johnnie, however, never knew his mother as a teacher.

When his mother was 16 and his father was 25, they got married. They were married approximately 15 years before they had any children. When his father died, it disrupted things, leaving his mother to raise four children alone. "My mother wasn't that strict, " John recalls, "but all four of us kids were disciplined. In those days, kids couldn't just lie around the house, we had to work and help support the family."

His siblings were Statia, Willis and Carroll, also known as "Buster". Statia was always reading. "She must have read every book in the school library," said Johnnie. In those days, girls had home economics classes where they learned how to sew and cook. Statia learned how to sew well and became a seamstress. She also made quilts and clothes.

His brother, Willis, was outgoing. He was the kind of guy everyone loved. He was taught to fly an airplane when he was 14 years of age by a man at an airport then located on NE 63rd and Bryant Street in Oklahoma City. He learned to play golf when he was no more than 10 or 12 years old. While Johnnie was still in high school, Willis left home; no one knew where he was for a long time. One day as the family was sitting outside; they saw a soldier coming down the road. They knew it was Willis from his distinctive walk; one of his legs was shorter than the other. Willis had joined the Army!

Willis was probably one of the first Black golfers in Oklahoma City. He learned to play golf by caddying. He taught himself how to play the guitar and later taught music.

Buster, Johnnie's youngest brother, would aggravate everyone in the house with his drumsticks even as a child. He was always beating on something ... a pot, a pan, a table, a chair, anything. Buster became a jazz musician, self-taught. At a young age, he played drums with some of the great musicians who came to Oklahoma City. Later he would travel to Detroit where John lived and eventually played with nationally known musicians in Detroit as well.

Unfortunately, Buster was killed in an

automobile accident and left behind a young son, Lawrence Peoples, who became a minister and pastor.

CHAPTER 3
GROWING UP

"It was the summer of 1947, during a church revival on a Sunday morning, that I accepted Christ as my Lord and Savior." —JWP

Johnnie had a wonderful time growing up in rural Oklahoma City. People walked everywhere they went. He got his first job at the age of seven, in 1941, during World War II. He worked for the only person he knew of at that time who had an automobile, Dr. Wyatt H. Slaughter.

Dr. Slaughter is credited as the first African American doctor in Oklahoma City. He had a multipurpose medical building located on the corner of Northeast 2nd and Styles Street. Dr. Slaughter also owned nearly 100 acres of farmland bordered by Northeast 50th Street on the South, Northeast 63rd Street on the North,

Bryant Street on the West and Vernon Road on the East. His house was a big rock structure, consisting of 16-18 rooms located at 3101 Northeast 50th Street.

It was on this farm that Johnnie met his first mentor, Mr. Charley Abernathy. He and his wife, Ruby, were overseers of Dr. Slaughter's farm. For Johnnie, losing his father at the age of two, Mr. Abernathy was like a surrogate father to him. He was about 25 years old and didn't have any children. "He would take me everywhere with him", John says smiling; "he would sit me in front of him on the wagon and let me hold the reigns and "drive" the horses which made me feel really good." Johnnie was always with him in all the work on the farm, chopping corn, seeing after chickens, turkeys and pigs. At 12 years of age, Johnnie was working eight hours per day and loving every minute of it.

Johnnie called Mr. Abernathy "daddy." He considered himself Mr. Abernathy's son and still does to this day!

When Johnnie was seven years old, Mr. Abernathy gave him a job. His job was to water the lawn for two hours every evening except Sunday, pull weeds out of Mrs. Slaughter's flower garden and feed the chickens. He was paid .25 an hour. That amounted to $3.00 for the six days he worked. Of course, he gave every penny to his mother.

When Johnnie was 12 years old, he worked on Dr. Slaughter's farm. Dr. Slaughter had several cows, horses, pigs, sheep, goats, chickens, ducks: every farm animal imaginable. There was at least 75 acres of grain such as corn, wheat, oats, and alfalfa hay, as well as every vegetable imaginable. When school was out for the summer Johnnie worked in the field "chopping corn." He was paid .50 per hour. By the end of the summer, he had earned enough money to buy some school clothes and a 10-speed bicycle. He paid $25.00 for the bicycle.

"I learned to ride horses," Johnnie ruminates, "this is where I learned a lot about life."

Johnnie would ride his bicycle two miles to Pilgrim Rest Baptist Church. It was the Summer of 1947, during a church revival on a Sunday morning, that John accepted Christ as his Lord and Savior.

Mr. Murray Butler, also the Sunday School Superintendent, owned a large farm about five miles from the church and about six or seven miles from where Johnnie lived. Mr. Butler also owned a large cattle watering tank. The cattle watering tank was the "baptismal pool" where Johnnie was baptized by the Reverend John H. Young, who at the time was the pastor of the church.

Johnnie remembers riding his bicycle immediately after church to Butler's farm to be baptized. He was baptized on the second Sunday of August, 1947, because that was the day set aside for baptizing. Johnnie remembers it being a hot Summer day. Several other children from the community were baptized that day too. Johnnie was baptized in the same pants and shirt that he had worn to church. Johnnie rode his bicycle, wet clothes and all, the entire distance from the Butler farm back to his home. His clothes were completely dry by the time he got home. When he told his mother that he had been baptized she was so happy.

CHAPTER 4
EDUCATION

"Seems like God picked me up and put me in that automotive class." —JWP

Johnnie started school in 1938, at the early age of four. He attended Harrison Elementary School, which was located on Sooner Road, just north of 63rd Street. Harrison Elementary School was four miles from where he lived.

The principal of Harrison was Mrs. Jennie Hill, who allowed Johnnie's mother to enroll him in school at that earlier than usual age because there was no one to look after him. His mother had to work to take care of her four children. At that time, the school bus stopped right in front of their house. However, during the Second World War (1941-1946), the school bus route was changed. When Johnnie was seven years of age, he had to walk a mile to catch the school bus. The school bus route was changed to save on gasoline because gasoline was rationed during the war.

At 14 years of age, Johnnie graduated from Harrison Elementary School and went on to attend Frederick Douglass High School; he was in the 9th grade. It was important during those days for children to work so they could help out at home. Johnnie proudly kept a job so he could help his mother with the bills. During his high school years, he worked at the cotton gin, at a bookstore and washed dishes at a restaurant in the downtown area.

When Johnnie was 15 years old and in the 10th grade, he bought his first car, a 1936 Ford. It was important back then for young men to learn a skill. They would put most of the boys in what was called "trade classes" so they would be able to get good jobs after graduation.

Initially, Johnnie was enrolled in a brick

masonry class. He had a friend, however, Morris Carolina, who was in an automotive class and Johnnie wanted to be in that class too. After being in the masonry class for a week, remarkably, Johnnie was transferred to the automotive class. Reflecting, Johnnie says, "Seems like God just picked me up and put me in that class." The automotive class instructor was Paul Strong who was from McAlister, Oklahoma. Mr. Strong's wife was Johnnie's music teacher at Frederick Douglass High School.

Johnnie studied auto mechanics for four years; 9th, 10th, 11th and 12th grades. He enjoyed this class very much and it was in this class, he found a home. Because he was interested and worked hard, he became a rather good mechanic and learned a lot. In fact, he and his friend did so well; at the end of the school year, his instructor entered them in a contest at Langston University. Young Black men from all over the state of Oklahoma, including Ardmore, Okmulgee, Muskogee, Tulsa and Lawton participated in this automotive contest.

The objective of this contest was for students to assemble an engine and make it run for at least three minutes. "Mr. Strong trained us well, teaching us how to work together as a team", says John. He would work underneath the automobile and Morris would work on top. The first part of the contest began in the morning. The students would take an engine apart and lay all the parts out. They would then take a written exam which lasted about an hour. After lunch, they would perform the second part of the contest. This included putting the engine back together. That first year it took Johnnie and his friend 23 minutes to put it back together and it ran for three minutes, giving them a total time of 26 minutes. They won first place. The second year, having gained some experience, they were able to cut the total time in half to 13 minutes, the engine running for three minutes. They won first place in the automotive contest in the state of Oklahoma for two years. Johnnie graduated from Frederick Douglass High School in 1952.

CHAPTER 5
AT A CROSSROAD

"I had a trade that I was good at and couldn't be hired because of the color of my skin." —JWP

In 1952, at 17 years of age, Johnnie graduated from Frederick Douglass High School. With two first place certificates in auto mechanics in hand, a letter of recommendation from Paul Strong, he was able to secure a job with Jack Strong, Paul's brother, who owned an auto mechanic shop on Lottie Avenue in Oklahoma City. While employed there, as a student, he learned two important things; how to organize and how to work neat and clean. Recalling this experience, Johnnie adds, "I was not a grease monkey, you would never see me with greasy clothes or greasy hands, I was immensely proud of this."

Johnnie decided he was now ready to

apply for a job in downtown Oklahoma City. He sought employment at a Packard Motor Car Company, a new car dealership on NW 11th and Robinson in Oklahoma City. With high school diploma in hand, letters of recommendation from his automotive teacher Mr. Paul Strong, Paul's brother Jack Strong; F.D. Moon, Principal of Douglass High School, and his counselor Mr. Jake Diggs, along with all of his vocational credentials, off he went.

When he arrived at the dealership to apply for a job as a mechanic helper, he was told by the service manager they didn't hire Colored boys for that position. But if he wanted to wash cars or work as a porter, he could, but he declined. Johnnie was devastated, he really wanted that job. He thought, I have worked hard. I have my high school diploma and credentials showing I have been trained in the field of auto mechanics; I have a trade that I am good at and couldn't be hired because of the color of my skin. He left that shop devastated and hurt.

He walked five miles home. While reflecting on this experience, Johnnie says, "I was so hurt, I cried because I really wanted to work as a mechanic's helper. After all these years, I still feel that hurt when I think about it."

On his long walk home from downtown Oklahoma City to 50th and Bryant, he cried. How could this be happening? He had done all the right things and was still turned down. During that long walk home, Johnnie made a decision which would change the trajectory of his life.

When he arrived home, he told his mother, "Mama, I'm leaving Oklahoma." His mother stopped what she was doing, looked at him and asked, "Where you going?" With a made-up mind, Johnnie said, "Mama, I'm going to Detroit." Looking at her son, confused, she exclaimed, "What are you going there for? You don't have no people in Detroit!" Listening to his mother, Johnnie said, "that's where they make cars and Mama, I believe I can get a job there as a mechanic. Mama, I want to go to Detroit."

Conceive and believe and make your dreams come true.

CHAPTER 6
THE LESSON

"I learned to never follow anyone and make my own decisions." —JWP

Johnnie didn't have the money to go to Detroit, but he was determined to go. He strongly believed he could get a job as an auto mechanic in Detroit.

In May 1952, the young 18 year-old Johnnie was on his way! He worked at Sonny's Groceries located at NE 5th and Eastern Avenue by day and at a restaurant at night in downtown Oklahoma City. He also worked at a bookstore on Robinson Street from May-September 1952 and managed to save $50.00 or $60.00.

He bought his first automobile in 1960, a 1936 Ford. This allowed him to drive to school and to his jobs.

He then decided to go to Wichita,

Kansas to find a job; some of the guys who attended Douglass with him were there.

He landed a job at Boeing Aircraft Company. He secured a room at a boarding house which was owned by a middle-aged couple. There were about 15 boys living at this boarding house.

John recalls an incident at work where he learned a valuable lesson. He and a friend went on their lunch break which was 30 minutes. They decided to go out on the strip, sit in their car and "people watch". They saw people go in and out of nightclubs enjoying themselves. They were having a good time as well sitting in their car talking and laughing. In fact, they were having such a good time; they were 60 minutes late returning to work. On returning to work, their boss met them at the door and said, "You boys know you were supposed to be back from lunch at 7:30 and here it is 8:30, and you just now coming back to work, so I'm gonna give you a warning, if you do this again, I'm gonna fire you." He then turned to his friend and asked, "Now how do you feel about that?" "Don't make no difference to me," his friend responded. He then turned to Johnnie and asked, "How do you feel about it young man?" Mimicking his friend, Johnnie replied, "Don't make me no difference either." Johnnie and his friend were fired at that very moment. Even though Johnnie didn't realize it at that time, he had learned a very important lesson which he never forgot. That lesson he learned was to never follow anybody and to make his own decisions.

His next job was in Wichita, Kansas. It was at the Cudahy Packing Plant which was a good paying job at that time. What a lot of people may not know is that there are a lot of flies and gnats at these plants. He says there were so many flies, he couldn't eat his lunch! He didn't like this job at all. His job was to sort out the skins of the animals which was a sticky job. He explains "My clothes would stick to me; my socks would stick to my feet and my legs stuck to my pants; I couldn't take it and I quit without receiving my pay." This job only lasted four or five days.

Johnnie then got what he described as a "very nice" job in downtown Wichita, where he worked at a women's store called "Lewins Ready to Wear Store". Mr. Lewins and Mr. Meriwether were good people who treated their employees well. In fact, they would send Johnnie to the bank to make the deposits for the store.

Mr. Meriweather had a Lionel race car train set in his home which really fascinated Johnnie. He wanted to know how it worked!

Johnnie left Kansas in December, 1952, with his mind set on Detroit.

CHAPTER 7
GOD SENDS ANGELS

"It was like heaven to me; here I am working in the place I have dreamed about!" —JWP

March 10, 1953, young Johnnie Peoples boarded a Greyhound bus with a one-way ticket to Detroit, Michigan and $30.00 in his pocket. He carried an elegant looking gray and green suitcase which his mom purchased for him exclusively for this journey. She also carefully packed a big box full of food which included pork chops, fried chicken and peanut butter and jelly sandwiches. In those days, African Americans could not eat in the bus terminals, or any other White owned place.

On boarding the Greyhound bus, he found it to be filled to capacity with passengers and he landed in the very back of the bus sandwiched between two heavy set women.

After 12-15 hours of uncomfortable riding in the bus, Johnnie finally arrived in Terre Haute, Indiana, where most of the people got off, including the two heavy set women who shared his seat. He decided this was a good time for him to get off the bus, stretch his legs, and get something cold to drink. He went into the bus station and bought a bottle of pop. When he got back on the bus, he noticed there were a lot of empty seats available. He also realized they had crossed the Mason Dixon Line (an imaginary line that geographically separated the North from the South) which meant he could now sit at the front of the bus. He took a wide seat, two or three seats from the front of the bus. At last, he had enough room to stretch out his legs and relax. He thought, now I can get some sleep!

At that very moment, he noticed a tall

slender Colored man boarding the bus. The man stopped and looked all over that bus. "Instead of taking one of those vacant seats", exclaimed Johnnie, "He took a seat next to me. This made me so angry, I didn't know what to do, I planned to sleep; and what was even worse is that this stranger wanted to talk to me," said Johnnie.

The man introduced himself to Johnnie and asked, "Young man, where you on your way to?" "Detroit," Johnnie replied. We traveled another few miles and this man again looked at me and asked, "where you from?" Johnnie replied, "Oklahoma City". We rode another 10 or 15 miles and he asked, "You going to see some of your relatives?" "No sir," said Johnnie. They rode on down the road a little more and once again the man turned to him and asked, "where you gonna live when you get to Detroit, you got any people in Detroit?" "Oh, I'll find a place," John responded. The bus continued down the road getting closer to Detroit and the man says, "Well, young man, I live in Saginaw, Michigan, but I got a friend in Detroit; I think I'll stop and see him." My newly found friend got off the bus and asked me to go to the telephone booth with him, and I did. He telephoned his friend and about 30 minutes later, his friend showed up. They embraced each other since they hadn't seen each other in quite a long time. His friend then took us to his house in Detroit. His wife prepared a big Thanksgiving type dinner or a Sunday dinner. We all sat there and ate.

Now this man had two sons about my age, and I began to talk with them. The two men talked for a long time; they were both from Arkansas. Johnnie says he remembers this man telling his sons to make room for him in their room because he would be spending the night.

I got up about seven the next morning and was told to get dressed. At this time, the two men and I left for the bus station.

We dropped off the man who was headed to Saginaw at the bus station. His friend took me all over the city of Detroit looking for a job. We went to General Motors, Chevrolet, the Dodge Main Plant, Plymouth, and a steel mill. I completed job applications at each plant but didn't get a job. It was around two o'clock by now. We went back to his house, where his wife prepared lunch for us.

The man then looked at me and said, "Come on young man, let's go out to Ford Motor Company." We arrived at Ford Motor Company about 4:30 PM. Johnnie filled out the application and the man said, "You have a nice handwriting, can you come back tonight for the midnight shift?" The man who took me there said, "Yes, he can come back!" John was then told to be at work about 10:30 PM. They went back to the man's house where John took a nap. The man's wife fixed a lunch for him. Later, the man drove him 15 miles to Ford Motor

Company, to his new job. En route to his job, the man explained to him how to catch the bus back to his house.

On walking into the Ford Motor Company that night, Johnnie describes it as, "It was like heaven to me; here I am working in the place I have dreamed about!" He was amazed at all the machines. He thought to himself, this is where they make the cars. Johnnie said, "I only wanted to be a mechanic and here I am, where they make the cars." He recalls not doing much work that first night. When his shift was over, he caught the bus back to the man's house. The man talked to him about his first night at work. He stayed at this man's house for two weeks until he made his first paycheck. Then the man took me to get a room at a lady's house who rented rooms for $10.00 per week and got me all situated.

CHAPTER 8
ANOTHER ANGEL

"Help comes from unexpected places." —JWP

Johnnie was now working midnights at the Ford Motor Company. He was amazed at what he had been able to accomplish in such a short time.

One night, as he stood in line to punch the time clock, an old White man standing behind him whom he describes as being from the "old country" (The "old country" meaning somewhere in Europe) suggested to him that he go to the employment office and apply for the apprenticeship program. "At that time", Johnnie said, "we were taught to obey White men."

In June, 1953, Johnnie went to the employment office, filled out the application for the apprenticeship program and took the test. Two months later, in August of 1953, his supervisor informed him he was to go to the employment office. He was then told by the personnel department he had been accepted into the apprenticeship program and was taken to his new work area.

Since starting his job at Ford Motor Company, Johnnie had been on a production job, doing the same thing over and over. In this new assignment at work, everything was about to change for him, including his name. In his new workplace, there were only two Black men and four or five White men. One of the Black men was told that Johnnie was his new apprentice. As Johnnie looked up at the Black guy, he could see tears in his eyes. He told John he was the first Black male to be accepted in this program and he had been on this job for 30 years. The Tool & Die Department is the most highly skilled department in the automotive industry. His new leader told Johnnie he was glad he had been accepted into the program.

At that time, John didn't know the significance of that!

He started out in the Maintenance Department, where safety was of the utmost importance. It wasn't unusual to see a finger missing on a worker's hand; it was dangerous!

Despite the danger involved, Johnnie was excited to be in this program working on machines. Johnnie was required to complete 32 courses and to be on the job for 8,000 hours over a period of four years. The first two classes were basic shop math and blueprint reading. After those two classes the course work became increasingly harder. Johnnie was required to complete Algebra 1, 2, and 3; Geometry 1, 2, and 3, Trigonometry 1, 2, and 3, Compound Angles 1 and 2, and then Gearing 1 and 2. He was required to complete a course in Heat Treating. He started out making $1.50 an hour which was a cut in pay from his previous $1.80 per hour. Every 1,000 hours of on-the-job training along with the completion of eight courses, he would get a five cent raise in pay. At the completion of the four-year apprenticeship program John was earning $2.00 per hour, and would receive a raise every few months until he reached the maximum hourly rate of $5.00 an hour. John worked as a Skilled Tradesman in the Tool and Die Department at the Ford Motor Company for several years.

CHAPTER 9
BUSINESS MINDED

"God has been so good to me all my life." —JWP

After working four years at the Ford Motor Company, and having completed the apprenticeship program, John did get laid off. He recalls during this time noticing there were houses in downtown Detroit where very wealthy people lived. He noticed underneath the houses were rather large garages, where people parked their cars, and above the garage was the living quarters.

One day, while riding around, he noticed a sign which said "For Rent" tacked onto one of the garages. He contacted the homeowner who was an attorney who agreed to rent him the garage. The house had a two-car garage. John's plan was to open an auto shop, and he did! He then went to a Sears and Roebuck and bought some hand tools, a jack and two safety stands. He made a sign which said, "Johnny's Garage". People in the neighborhood brought their cars to him for minor repairs.

By this time, it was the early 1960's, Dwight Eisenhower was president. Eventually he was called back to work on the midnight shift. This worked out fine because he could work in his garage during the day. However, he ended up being laid off again.

This is what happened. He remembers driving home from work one morning (He worked the midnight shift at Ford's) with lay off papers in hand. He remembers vividly stopping at a stop light at Joy Road and Dexter. He looked to his right and saw a big, almost new Mobil service station with the flying red horse. Upon looking in the window, he saw a for-lease sign. As soon as he got home, he called Mobil Oil

Company. He was told to come down to their office at 906 West Grand Boulevard. He ended up being there all day, telling them about all his accomplishments. Finally, he was told he was a good candidate and would need about $10,000 to get in. He was then asked how much money he had. John had saved $1,000.00. John knew he couldn't give up all of his money, so he told the man he had $900.00. The man told him he would see what he could do. On returning, he told John they did have a program and because of his outstanding background, they could put in everything he needed to operate the business. They would put in 10,000 gallons of gasoline, several cases of oil, fan belts, water hoses, fuel and air filters, tires, batteries and a few other accessories. They would provide everything he needed. He then told John how the program worked. At that time, gasoline was selling at 20 cents a gallon, but he would get it for

10 cents a gallon. In that way, John would make 10 cents for every gallon sold. He went on to further explain the business plan to John. This plan proved to be quite lucrative for the 22 year old John.

John says, "God has been so good to me all my life."

John says has never been extravagant, and he learned how to save; this he has tried to instill in his kids as well as young people of today. He says he has been so blessed for the men God has put in his life to guide him.

While John was operating his service station, he still worked the midnight shift at Ford Motor Company.

The sign over the door of the Mobile gasoline station was Peoples Mobil Service.

It is believed that it was around this time he began referring to himself as John W. Peoples.

CHAPTER 10
AN UNEXPECTED CALL
EDUCATION

"I finally made up my mind to apply for a job in education." — JWP

John recalls a customer, Ms. Ann Evans, one of his customers at his service station who worked at Detroit Public Schools. She would come in to have her car serviced about once a month. During these visits she would tell him he should apply for a job at Detroit Public Schools. She continued to tell him this for about four years. Finally, one day, he made up his mind. The next time Ms. Evans came to have her car serviced; he would be able to tell her he had applied for a job with the Detroit Public School System.

John went to apply for a job and was

scheduled for an interview with the Director of Vocational Education. At this time, Detroit had just built three brand new high schools. Each of these schools offered different trades. During the interview he was informed the three schools would be opening in September. They wanted one of the schools to have an automotive service program. They went on to say they wanted their instructors to have experience; in fact, they emphasized the importance of experience since the instructor would set up this program at the high school.

This was in June of 1965. In August, he made a visit to Oklahoma City to visit his mother. While he was there, he got a call from the Director of the Vocational Educational Department of Detroit Public Schools. He was informed to be at the school for orientation a week before Labor Day.

John immediately left Oklahoma City to

go back to Detroit to prepare for this job. He completed his orientation.

His first day on the job as an instructor at Kettering High School, he recalls nothing being in the classroom for the students; no desks, no chairs, no chalkboards, no paper or pencils, no supplies of any kind. He had 30 students walk into his classroom on the first day wanting to study auto mechanics. John had to develop a curriculum. Even though he had never been to college and had no degree, here he was a teacher!

He was informed that he would be required to go to college and get just eight credit hours a year in order to keep the teaching job. He had to pray about this. Was this something he really wanted to do? After all, he had his service station and was still working at the Ford Motor Company. John's plate was full! His director informed him, he didn't have to settle for eight credit hours, he could get a degree.

With his mind made up, John started college in 1965 and continued for 15 long years, earning a Bachelor of Science, Master of Education, an Education Specialist and the Doctor of Education degrees.

When John sat for the doctorate degree examination, he was told the process would last approximately six hours and he should bring a lunch. The process began with him taking a two-hour written exam. He was then questioned for three hours in defending his dissertation. Finally, he was asked to leave the room and told they would call him back in when they were ready. Although he had brought his lunch, he was unable to eat. He nervously sat outside the room for about 30 minutes. When he was called back into the room, Dr. Tommie Johnson, the chairperson of the doctoral examination committee, looked at him and said, "Congratulations,

Dr. Peoples."

Words cannot express what he felt at that moment. John had been going to school for 15 long years! He simply said, "I cried."

CHAPTER 11
CALLED TO PREACH
THE GOSPEL

"I was called to preach the gospel of Jesus Christ." —JWP

In 1961, John acknowledged the call to preach the gospel of Jesus Christ, and in 1965, John was called to pastor the Union Baptist Church in rural Chatham Ontario, Canada.

One day, a gentleman came by his service station because his car had broken down. On finding out John was a young minister; he mentioned to John they needed someone to pastor a church in Chatham, Ontario, Canada. At that time, he told the man, he may be interested. Arrangements were made for him to go to Canada to seek out this opportunity. He was to meet with a deacon, Herb Simmons.

On the first Saturday afternoon of

August around 3:30 PM, he arrived in Chatham. He found the house of Herb Simmons. No one was at home. There was a lady across the street that was very friendly. People in Canada are quite friendly. John introduced himself to the lady. The lady asked if he was looking for Herb Simmons. He told her yes and she told him he was out in Dresden, which she referred to as the country. She then asked if he would be interested in going out in the country where Mr. Simmons was; John responded yes. They then got in the car and headed for the country. The trip was about 15 miles on a dirty dusty road.

Upon arriving in Dresden and meeting Mr. Simmons, he was informed they had a preacher for the upcoming Sunday, but asked could he come back the next Sunday. He said yes.

The following Sunday, August 1965, he returned to Chatham. Traveling down a gravel road, he had difficulty finding the church and didn't find it until around 11:15 AM; worship was to have started at 11:00 AM. At last, He saw the name of the church and a man directed him to the church parking lot. When he pulled into the parking lot, the man parked the car for him.   When John saw the building, he thought, I know I don't want to be pastor of this old church! It was a very small one room building. It was an old building with homemade pews and a wooden floor. In the middle of the floor, there was a pot-belly stove used for heating the building. The chimney of the stove went up to the ceiling, and through the roof of the building.

The people in the church were as quiet as a mouse. John knew he didn't want to be there.   He was introduced to the congregation. The interesting thing that happened was they asked John to come back. He let them know he was going on vacation and when he could return, and he did. From that day on and for the next 11 years, never missing a Sunday, he pastored that church. He felt that was where God wanted him to be. The people did too. They told him they had been waiting for God to send them a pastor and felt God had sent him.

Within two years, we built a completely new church. We tore down the old building because the new church was to be built there. We literally worshiped in a barn which had been there since 1865. At that time, in the upper part of the barn, the hay was kept and the lower part is where the horses were kept. There were steps going up to the upper part and this was converted into a place of worship while the church was being built. Through my leadership, it took approximately five months for the new church to be completed.

I found out that one of the members was a builder and had built many houses in that area. In addition to that both of his sons were in the same business; one was a brick mason and the other a carpenter. We already had the people we needed to build the new church. God was working it out! They were able to get the carpentry work done. We did have to hire an electrician and a plumber.

The happiest time for the people in the church was the day we went in and dedicated that church. Some of them had been in the church all their lives. Some were in their 80's; one lady was in her 90's. They had been in that church; that one room building, all their lives with that pot-bellied stove and wood floors. Someone had made the benches.

It has been 50 years and there is still a close connection between the people who are left in that church and John. Most of the people who are still there now were children when John was there. They all think there is no one like John.

Through my leadership, it took approximately five months for the new church to be completed.

John recalls how he would go to Chatham every Saturday, spend the night in preparation for church services on Sunday. The trip was approximately 150 miles round trip.

John was now pastor at the church in Chatham, Canada, teacher at Kettering High School in Detroit, Michigan, had his own business and was still employed at Ford Motor Company.

Although John had been ordained as a preacher of the gospel by his pastor, the Reverend Lawler Juan Burt, who was pastor of the Calvary Baptist Church of Detroit, at the request of the Reverend Joseph Sutton who was pastor of the New St. Paul Baptist church where John had been serving as assistant to Pastor Sutton, the Union Baptist of Dresden, Ontario, Canada required John to be ordained by a

Canadian church. He was ordained in Canada by the Reverend Mac Brown who was pastor of the First Baptist Church of Windsor, Ontario, Canada.

John commuted 150 miles each Sunday to and from this church for 11 years. While serving the 30 member congregation, a completely new place of worship was built. The old Union Baptist Church building was over 100 years old, having been built in the mid 1800's. Under the leadership of Pastor John Peoples, a completely new building was constructed in 1968, valued at $150,000. The congregation also grew from 30 members to 200 members.

CHAPTER 12
CALVARY BAPTIST CHURCH

"I was called to serve my home church in Detroit."
—JWP

John was pastor at the church in Chatham, Canada, teacher at Kettering High School in Detroit and working at Ford Motor Company. He now decides to attend seminary school in Wilberforce, Ohio. This meant he had to give up the job at Ford Motor Company. He had already gone to Wayne State University in Detroit to certify himself as a teacher. He only needed eight hours to keep his provisional certificate. However, he also had to give up his job as teacher and he was allowed to take a leave from teaching for three years.

In the meantime, he had also been called to his home church, Calvary Baptist

Church in Detroit. Urban Renewal was taking place and Calvary Baptist Church had been purchased by the city of Detroit. This church was a historic building in Detroit. Urban Renewal was wiping out a lot of churches at that time. John's pastor had fought against selling the church, but ultimately had to sell.

The pastor died two months after the church was sold. This church had been there for 60 or 70 years, a historic church in Detroit. They had nowhere to worship. The church was given 90 days to find another location. They started looking right away for another church. They decided they might as well look in that same area. They found two acres near Elmwood Cemetery, a historic cemetery in Detroit. After negotiation, they were able to purchase the property.

In 1978, they marched into this new church at 1000 McDougall Street. They negotiated $1.3 million dollars to build the church. The church was unique; people thought it was a Howard Johnson because there were mirrors all over the church. The architectural idea behind this was being in the church you needed to see yourself standing before God. The outside of the church had clear windows, designed so as the community could see you. The interpretation was that just as you could see yourself, God could also see you.

The carpet was green, referencing the 23rd Psalm.

CHAPTER 13
POLITICS

"I never thought of myself as being a politician." —JWP

Dr. Charles W. Butler, pastor of New Calvary Baptist Church, a Morehouse College graduate. He was the most theologically in-depth person John had ever known. He taught John a lot. Dr. Butler had studied and taught Hebrew and Greek. When he started speaking, he had everyone's attention and he didn't even have a whoop!

Around 1980, just before one of John's Progressive National conventions, John learned one of the city councilmen of Detroit had died. While visiting the Butler's home, Dr. Butler's wife, Helen, approached him and said, "Peoples, why don't you run for City Councilman, you're a young intelligent man." John told her he never thought about being a politician and knew nothing about politics. She told him he could learn! Ms. Butler went and picked up the petitions from the election commission. They would need to have 1,000 signatures. While John was attending the convention, Mrs. Butler and Mrs. Ruby Davis was out collecting signatures for the petition. It took the two of them just one week to collect the needed signatures. Davis then took the petitions to the Election Commission. They notified him, letting him know he was approved to run as a candidate. John asked, "So, now what do I do?" John was told he needed a committee and some money. In fact, he needed $50,000 which he did not have. They organized a campaign committee and put together a fundraiser. One of the ministers loaned the committee $25,000. John was a member of the Council of Baptist Pastors of Detroit; there were about 400 of them.

Each of these pastors asked their church for a donation to John's campaign. They had many fundraisers. He ultimately ended up coming in number 12 out of the 18 who qualified in the primary election. John got out there and campaigned hard! He jokingly says, "I didn't know how to campaign, but I knew how to preach." His campaign slogan was, I'm concerned, I'm committed and I'm capable.

John was elected as a City Councilman for the City of Detroit. This was in 1981. The job paid $42,000 a year. As City Councilman, he had access to a car and all expenses were covered by the city. They supplied gas for his car and even washed the car once a week. He received lots of gifts during the holidays from different businesses.

At this point, he had a lot on his plate, being a pastor, teacher at Kettering High School and attending Wayne State University. He decided to continue teaching, however. During this time several people approached him about running for Mayor of Detroit. He had to decide. Would he get completely involved in politics or would he pastor? John was accustomed to making hard decisions. He says he believed he had a good chance of winning the mayoral position because he was a radio and television producer and personality, and a lot of people knew him. However, he decided to follow Jesus. He says he also had an opportunity to become a Congressman. George Crockett, who was a prominent lawyer in Detroit and retiring U. S. Congressman endorsed him. John chose to follow Jesus!

CHAPTER 14
AN UNEXPECTED TURN

"Everyone who wants me to be your pastor,
please stand." —JWP

John stayed in education and in the church. He became an administrator in one of the five Vocational Technical Centers in Detroit. The Centers had been mandated by a federal judge that the City of Detroit had to build five Vocational Technical Centers to train the young people of Detroit and help them to acquire skills. He was an administrator at the A. Phillip Randolph Vocational Technical School. John retired from the Detroit Public School's in 2003.

John resigned from the 600 member Calvary congregation in 1989. He was then Called to the smaller Cosmopolitan Baptist Church in Detroit in 1990 and served the

Cosmopolitan congregation until 2003.

John would visit with his sister, Statia and other relatives in Oklahoma City every year. When in Oklahoma City, John would often meet with the Reverend T. J. Roberts, pastor of Evangelistic Church. On this particular Saturday morning, while Pastor Roberts and John were having breakfast together, Pastor Roberts received a phone call. He was reminded that he had a meeting with a group of ministers who were assisting a church in getting a pastor, and told John he had to leave immediately. As they were leaving the restaurant and getting into their cars Pastor Roberts got out of his car and came over to John's car and asked, "Peoples, didn't you tell me you just retired?" John responded, "yes." Pastor Roberts then said, "Peoples, you are the man, I am going to put your name in."

A few weeks later, John received a call from a Deacon Watson of the Faith Memorial Baptist Church and was extended an invitation to come preach at their church; John accepted the invitation. After preaching John was asked by Deacon Watson to come back and preach the next Sunday. John called his church in Detroit and told them he would be in Oklahoma City another week.

Before he left Oklahoma City, a group of the church leaders met with him and interviewed him for about an hour. Notably, John had not applied for a pastoral position.

He returned to Detroit and soon received a call from one of the leaders of Faith Memorial Baptist Church. He was told he had been elected to pastor their church. Still being pastor of the Cosmopolitan Church in Detroit, he had to give this offer some serious thought.

A few weeks later John returned to Oklahoma City and preached at the Faith Memorial Baptist Church. John told the congregation he realized they had voted for him to pastor their church. However, he had to see for himself. He asked that everyone who wanted him to pastor their church to stand up. Almost everyone in the church stood up. Now John had to make a big decision. He had spent most of his life in Detroit, everything was there!

He prayed and put everything in God's hand. He accepted the position. This meant he had to uproot. He had been in Detroit for over 50 years. John left Oklahoma City when he was 17 years old. Everything had changed about Oklahoma City.

He moved back to Oklahoma City. He had to stay in a hotel for three weeks. One day while driving, he ran into a housing district that was built in 1949, Forest Park. He found out the lady who owned the house had recently lost her husband and was selling the house. The house sat on two acres off the road and wasn't far from where I was raised as a child.

CHAPTER 15
HOME AGAIN

"Out of sadness rivers of water flowed from the eyes of the three congregations I served." —JWP

John purchased the property and relocated to his birthplace after having lived in Detroit for 50 years. John, as a pastor, was instrumental in leading two different congregations in building a completely new place of worship: the Union congregation in Dresden, Ontario, Canada and the Calvary congregation in Detroit, Michigan. John led the Cosmopolitan congregation of Detroit in purchasing additional property and plans were being developed for constructing a new place of worship and a small shopping strip.

Upon John announcing to the Cosmopolitan congregation that he had accepted a new charge in Oklahoma City, even though it was the place of his birth, there was not a dry eye in the sanctuary. The same was true when John announced to the Union congregation in Dresden, Ontario, Canada as well as when he announced to the Calvary congregation in Detroit. But not only were rivers of water flowing from the eyes of the members of the three congregations where John had served, but oceans of water flowed from the eyes of John.

At the time of this writing John is in the 19th year of serving as pastor of the Faith Memorial Baptist Church congregation.

ACKNOWLEDGMENTS

I wish to acknowledge and express my deepest love and admiration to my wife, Alice, and her children Monique, Monte, Melanie. I also acknowledge, in memoriam, the following people whose influence on the very early years of my life, and even into the young adult years of my life, molded, formed shaped and instilled in me the values that have sustained me for my entire life.

CHARLIE ABERNATHY

Mr. Abernathy and his wife Ruby informally adopted me as their son when I was two years old. Mr. Abernathy was the only man I ever knew as a father; in fact, I called him "daddy" until he passed when I was 12 years of age. I refer to him even to this day as "daddy".

Paul Strong

Mr. Strong was my automotive mechanics instructor for the four years that I attended Frederick Douglass High School in Oklahoma City, Oklahoma. Douglass was the only high school in Oklahoma City for African Americans. Mr. Strong became my lifelong mentor and friend until he passed away at nearly 100 years of age.

Lucius "Slim" Ryan

I was introduced to Slim on the very first day that I became a Machine Repair Apprentice in the Tool and Die Department at the Ford Motor Company. I was among the first group of African American young men to be placed on an apprentice program at the Ford Motor Company, and would become a journeyman upon successfully completing the four-year apprenticeship. I remember Slim actually shedding tears when I was introduced to him as his apprentice. Slim had worked for more than 20 years as a machine repairman "upgrader", but being an African American he was never recognized as a journeyman as were the White workers who had much less knowledge, experience or seniority. And by the way, he never received the higher rate of pay as they did.

WILLIAM "BILL" MARSHALL

Bill Marshall became my mentor after I became a journeyman. Within less than a year as a journeyman I was transferred to Ford's Glass Plant where I met Bill Marshall. Marshall, like Ryan, also had 20 or more years of seniority as a machine repair "upgrader" but was never classified as a journeyman. Although 20 or more White men who were considered journeymen had to rely on Marshall as an "upgrader" because he was the best repairman in the entire department. When Ford management made the decision to relocate the Glass manufacturing operation to a completely new plant in Indianapolis, Indiana, Marshall was asked by management to take nine machine repairmen to Indianapolis to set-up the new plant. Although I had just recently graduated from the apprenticeship program and was a journeyman, although only 22 years old, Marshall asked me to go with him and the others who, by the way, were all White men.

Ann Evans

Ms. Evans was one of my regular customers for the entire time that I owned and operated the Peoples Mobil Gasoline and Automotive Service Station. It was Ms. Evans who continued to encourage me to apply to the Detroit Public Schools' for a teaching position. Feeling reluctant to do so because I knew that I did not have a college degree, so why bother. However, just so that I could say to her that I had applied I decided to do so. When I went to apply, the Director of the Vocational Department, after reviewing my credentials, informed me that the school system was opening three new schools in September and they needed an automotive service instructor. He hired me right on the spot, and I was assigned to Kettering Senior High School. I remained with the school system until I retired in 2003.

WILLIAM "BILL" JONES

Mr. William Jones was the principal at Kettering high school. Jones granted me a three year leave from my position as the automotive technology instructor at Kettering High School so that I could attend Payne Theological Seminary at Wilberforce, Ohio. Upon receiving the Master of Divinity degree from Payne Seminary I returned to my teaching position at Kettering High School. However, Mr. Jones appointed me as the Detroit Public Schools' Coordinator of the

Kettering Alternative Education Program, where I worked in cooperation with the Reverend Dr. Leon Sullivan, who established the Opportunities Industrial Center (OIC).

DR. ED WALKER

Dr. Ed Walker was my Doctoral Advisor at Wayne State University, and also served as the Chairman of the Doctoral Examination Committee along with six other committee members. Dr. Walker was not only my doctoral advisor he also owned an automotive repair service, and I was an automotive repair teacher. Dr. Walker had an open-door policy for me to bring my dissertation drafts to his service facility and his home for review or corrections. The final draft was presented, defended and approved by the Doctoral Examination Committee.

DR. TOMMIE JOHNSON

Dr. Johnson, an African American female, and the only female to serve on my Doctoral Examination Committee was especially helpful to me. The examination was a four hour, long, grueling, and stressful oral examination. In defense of my dissertation, I was questioned by five, White, male professors at Wayne State University. I was then asked to leave the room where the questioning had taken place. After 30 or more minutes Dr. Johnson was the first person to address me as "Dr. Peoples" as she informed me that I had successfully passed the oral doctoral examination.

My Call to Ministry

I would be remiss if I did not acknowledge the people who were especially helpful when I acknowledged my Call to become a preacher. They were as follows:

Reverend Allen Cox

The Reverend Allen Cox, who at the time was my father-in-law, was also the Pastor of the Union Baptist Church in Detroit where I attended church. Union Baptist Church was housed in a "store front." Reverend Cox helped me to understand what I believed to be a Call from God to become a preacher of the gospel of Jesus Christ; that was 60 years ago. Reverend Cox believed that I needed more exposure and of course formal training. His wise counsel, tutoring and advice led me to the next level.

Reverend Lawler Juan Burt

Reverend Burt was the pastor of the Calvary Baptist Church in Detroit. After uniting with the Calvary Church, I became a pulpit associate minister and helper to Pastor Burt. Pastor Burt was a Morehouse College trained minister and my first tutor. It was Pastor Burt who privately tutored me and encouraged me to accept the Call to my first pastorate in the rural area of Dresden, Ontario, Canada in 1966.

THE UNION BAPTIST CHURCH DRESDEN, ONTARIO, CANADA

The Union Church was a one-room building that had been built, including the pews and the pulpit, in 1885 by former slaves, many of whom had escaped from slavery in the United States and relocated in Canada. After being inducted as pastor of the Union Church by the Reverend Mack Brown, who was the President of the Amherstburg Baptist Association of Southwest Ontario, Rev. L. Juan Burt preached my Installation Sermon. It was at the Union Church where I led the congregation in the building of a completely new and modern house of worship. Pastor Burt died a few years after I began my pastorate at the Union Church.

Dr. Jacob C. Oglesby

While in search of another pastoral mentor after the death of pastor Burt, I had an occasion to meet Dr. Oglesby. Dr. Oglesby was the pastor of the Greater Christ Baptist Church in Detroit. Dr. Oglesby was also one of the professors serving at the Payne Theological Seminary in Wilberforce, Ohio, and who commuted from Detroit to Wilberforce each week. I had completed the bachelor's degree and the master's degree at Wayne State University. Dr. Oglesby encouraged me to enroll in the Master of Divinity program at Payne. In order for me to attend seminary in Ohio it was necessary for me to commute from Detroit to Wilberforce each week, a distance of 400 miles round-trip, as Dr. Oglesby was doing. But in my case, I was still pastoring the Church in Canada which is 150 miles round-trip from Detroit, and teaching at the Kettering High School in Detroit. I commuted these 550 miles each week.

Reverend Reuben Simpkins

Reverend Simpkins was serving as the Acting pastor at the Cosmopolitan Baptist Church in Detroit. Reverend Simpkins also served as one of my community liaison persons while I was serving as a Detroit City Councilman. Simpkins introduced and recommended me to the Cosmopolitan Baptist congregation whose pastor had recently passed away. I was Called to serve as pastor of the Cosmopolitan congregation and served for 11 years. Although Reverend Simpkins passed away before I was called to the Faith Memorial Baptist Church congregation in Oklahoma City, Oklahoma, we remained good friends until his death.

Lifelong Friends

There are so many other people that I have met, and who have been equally as instrumental in my journey through life. I wish now to mention a few: The Late Mr.

Jack Simons, also a Machine Repair Journeyman at the Ford Motor Company, Mr. Charles Robinson, the first African American Pattern Maker Journeyman at the Ford Motor Company and the first in the history of the United States. Mr. Clarence Cox, my former brother-in-law and friend, and Mr. Burt Lowe, both Skilled Trades Supervisors at the Ford company, and also life-long friends.

The Political Arena

COLEMAN A. YOUNG
Coleman A. Young was the first African American Mayor of the City of Detroit, and the longest serving Mayor of the City. Mayor Young played a major role in helping me to be elected to the Detroit City Council where I served for eight years.

REVEREND NICHOLAS HOOD
The Reverend Nicholas Hood, the longest

serving member of the Detroit City Councilman at the time, and who became my mentor in City government. I was elected to the Detroit City Council in 1981 and served until 1990. Whereas Reverend Hood was also the pastor of the Christian Church, actually tutored, and I was the pastor of the Calvary Baptist Church we were both colleagues in pastoral ministry as well as colleagues in city government. Reverend Hood helped me to understand how to be an effective servant of the people in the church and the citizens in the city at the same time.

ERMA HENDERSON

Erma Henderson was the first African American woman to be elected to the Detroit City Council. Councilwoman Henderson also served for several years as the President of the Council. Both Councilman Nicolas Hood and Councilwoman Henderson helped me to understand the governmental process.

Churches Were I Served

UNION BAPTIST CHURCH

I was called to serve as pastor of the Union Baptist Church in Dresden, Ontario, Canada in 1966 and served until 1975. I acknowledge all the members and we have remained close friends even to this day. While serving as Pastor at the Union Church, I also commuted and attended the Payne Theological Seminary in Wilberforce, Ohio. I acknowledge every member of the Union Church.

CALVARY BAPTIST CHURCH

I was Called to serve as pastor of the Calvary Baptist Church in Detroit, Michigan in 1976. Prior to being Called as pastor of the Calvary Baptist Church the City of Detroit was engaged in Urban Renewal and purchased the original Calvary Baptist Church building. Within a few months after the City purchased the

Calvary property Pastor Burt died. However, prior to Pastor Burt's death he and the church leaders had acquired about an acre of land in the Urban Renewal area. After the congregation had Called, and two different pastors during a two year period after Pastor Burt's death, I was Called to serve as an Interim Pastor. At the time I was attending Payne Theological Seminary in Wilberforce, Ohio. After graduating from seminary, I was installed as the pastor of the Calvary Baptist Church. I served during the construction of a $1.5 million dollar place of worship structure and led the congregation into the new house of worship on Easter Sunday in 1978. I served the Calvary congregation until 1988. I acknowledge every member of the Calvary congregation, and we are treasured friends even now.

COSMOPOLITAN BAPTIST CHURCH DEACON ROY BRADFORD AND HIS WIFE MRS. ORMA BRADFORD

Deacon Bradford was the Chairman of Deacons at the Cosmopolitan Baptist Church where I served for eleven years. Mrs. Bradford later became a Deaconess. The Bradford's are treasured friends even to this day. I acknowledge every member of the Cosmopolitan Church.

FAITH MEMORIAL BAPTIST CHURCH

I acknowledge Robert Dean, (Ret. Col.) current Chairman of Deacons and Senior Deacon Roy Watson who also served from time to time as Chairman. I also acknowledge Deacon Eugene Maclin who contacted and informed me that I had been selected as the pastor of Faith Memorial Baptist Church. I also acknowledge the other Deacons including Ed Williams, Garland Taylor, and Lawrence Pernell, and

Josh Robinson. I acknowledge current Trustee Chairperson Mrs. Cheryl Williams, and in memoriam Thelma Parks. I acknowledge all of the members of the Faith Memorial Baptist Church.

A Word of Thanks

KATHLEEN WATKINS
This book would never have been completed without the wise council, patience, encouragement, and support of Kathleen Watkins. Ms. Watkins, an Author, Playwright, and Founder of a local Theater Group, Spiritually Bold Inc.

THE EDITOR
Karen Redlack

THE COVER AND BOOK DESIGNER
Maurice Johnson of Self Publish Me, LLC

About the Author

Dr. John W. Peoples is a native of Oklahoma City, Oklahoma. After graduating from Frederick Douglass High School in Oklahoma City he relocated to Detroit, Michigan.

John W. Peoples is Well Educated
He holds the following credentials from Wayne State University, Detroit, MI.: D.Ed., Education Specialist Certificate, M. Ed., and the B.S. He also holds the M.Div. from Payne Theological Seminary, Wilberforce, Ohio.

John W. Peoples is a Pastor
He serves as pastor of the Faith Memorial Baptist Church, Oklahoma City, OK. (2003 to the current date (2021). He has served as a pastor at the Cosmopolitan Baptist Church, Det., MI., (1990-2003), The Calvary Baptist Church of Detroit, MI. (1976-1987), and the Union Baptist Church, Chatham, Ontario, Canada (1965-1976).

John W. Peoples is an Educator
and Community Servant

He worked as an Adjunct Teacher at the Ecumenical Theological Center, Detroit, MI. (1990-1991); Detroit Public Schools' Administrator at the A. Philip Randolph Vocational Technical Center (1992-2003), Community Relations Coordinator (1990-1991). He developed and taught the automobile mechanics course at Kettering High School, Detroit, MI. (1965-1982). Dr. Peoples also served as a Detroit City Councilman (1982-1989).

John W. Peoples is a Business Owner
and Skilled Tradesman

He owned Peoples Automobile Service from 1960 to 1965 while continuing to work as a Skilled Trades Machine Repair Journeyman in the Tool and Die Department, Ford Motor Company, Dearborn, MI. (1953-1965).

Dr. Peoples is a Husband, Father and Grandfather
Peoples has three biological children, Marlon, Roslyn and John W., III. He has one grandson, Donovan Peoples-Jones. Dr. Peoples is married to the former Alice M. White and they live in Oklahoma City, Oklahoma.

Dr. Peoples Motto is: *Service with Excellence*

Made in the USA
Columbia, SC
14 February 2023

12056078R00067